MW01502890

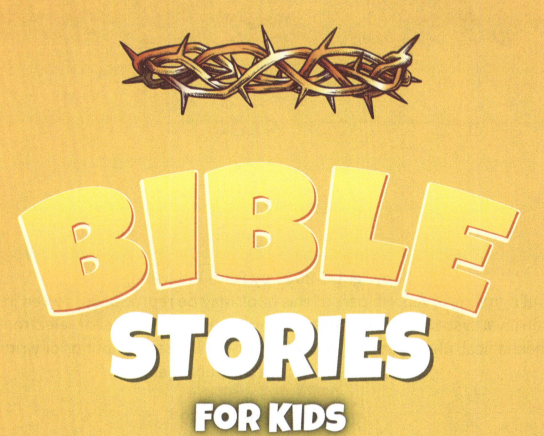

BIBLE
STORIES
FOR KIDS

Timeless Tales of Faith and Courage

Copyright © 2023 by Faith Publishing

All rights reserved. No part of this book may be reproduced, stored in a retrieval system, or transmitted in any form or by any means, electronic, mechanical, photocopying, recording, or otherwise, without prior written permission from the publisher.

ISBN: 9798865749509

INTRODUCTION

Welcome to a collection of 30+ captivating tales from the Bible, lovingly crafted for children. These stories will transport young readers on a remarkable journey through the pages of the most treasured book in history, revealing the timeless wisdom, courage, and compassion found within its sacred pages.

In these pages, your children will meet extraordinary characters like Noah, David, Ruth, and Jesus, and they'll explore stories of faith, friendship, and miracles. Each story is a beautiful reminder of the enduring values that guide our lives and the love that surrounds us. With engaging narratives, vibrant illustrations, and a focus on biblical accuracy, this book aims to instill a deep sense of spirituality and morality in the hearts of young readers. Each story is followed by a valuable lesson, making this book not just an adventure through the Bible but also a source of guidance for life's journey.

May these stories ignite a lifelong love for the Bible, nurturing the faith and understanding of your children. As you read and share these tales together, may they find inspiration, hope, and a stronger connection to the divine.

Let the adventure begin!

Jesus

TABLE OF CONTENTS

Jesus

In The Beginning

Genesis 1:1-31, 2:1-3

God's Creative Masterpiece

In the beginning, there was nothing but darkness and silence. But then, God spoke, "Let there be light," and there was light. God saw that the light was good, so He separated it from the darkness. He called the light "day" and the darkness "night."

On the second day, God created the sky, and He called it the heavens. He filled it with fluffy clouds and the endless beauty of the blue sky.

On the third day, God said, "Let the waters gather in one place, and let dry ground appear." He called the dry ground "land" and the gathered waters "seas." God created plants and trees of all kinds, each with their own seeds to grow more.

On the fourth day, God hung the sun, moon, and stars in the sky. They lit up the day and the night, helping us mark the seasons and years.

On the fifth day, God filled the seas and skies with living creatures. He made fish to swim in the water and birds to soar in the air. They filled the world with their beauty and songs.

On the sixth day, God created all the land animals, from tiny ants to the mighty elephants. He crafted them all with love and care. Then, God made something very special. He said, "Let us make mankind in our image." And so, God created Adam and Eve, the first people.

God looked at everything He had made, and it was very good. On the seventh day, He rested and blessed that day, making it holy.

Lesson: The story of creation reminds us of the incredible power and love of God. He created the world and everything in it, including you and me. It's a beautiful world, and we should take care of it. We should also remember that God made us in His image, so each one of us is unique and special.

Noah's Ark

Genesis 6-9

A Tale of Faith and the Great Flood

A long time after God created the world, people became very wicked and forgot about Him. But there was one good man named Noah who still loved and obeyed God. God saw Noah's faithfulness and decided to save him and his family.

God said to Noah, "Build an ark, a big boat. I will send a great flood to wash away all the wickedness from the earth, but you and your family will be safe inside the ark." So, Noah started building the ark with the help of his family.

The ark was huge, and it took many years to build. Noah followed God's instructions carefully. He built it with three floors and filled it with animals, two by two – a male and a female of each kind. The animals marched into the ark, guided by God, and they lived together peacefully.

When the ark was ready, the rain started. It poured down for forty days and forty nights, and the whole earth was covered with water. But inside the ark, Noah and his family were safe and dry.

Finally, the rain stopped, and the waters began to go down. Noah sent out a dove, and it came back with a fresh olive leaf, a sign that there was dry land. Soon, the ark landed on a mountain, and Noah and his family came out.

God made a promise to Noah and to all of us. He said, "I will never again send such a flood to destroy the earth." To remind us of this promise, God placed a rainbow in the sky.

Lesson: Noah's story teaches us about trust and obedience to God. Even when everyone else was doing wrong, Noah chose to do what was right and trusted God's plan. We learn that God keeps His promises and cares for those who follow Him.

The Tower of Babel

Genesis 11

Reaching for The Sky

Long after the time of Noah and the great flood, people came together to build a magnificent city. They were proud and determined to construct a towering monument that would reach up to the heavens. Their goal was to make a name for themselves and avoid being scattered across the vast earth.

As they worked tirelessly on the colossal tower, they were driven by their own ambitions, not considering God's plan for their lives. God saw their pride and the dangerous path they were following. He said to Himself, "If they are allowed to complete this tower, there's no telling what they will do next."

In response to their pride, God decided to intervene. He confused their language, causing the people to speak in different tongues. What was once a united effort turned into chaos, as they could no longer understand each other. This confusion forced them to stop building the tower.

Frustrated and bewildered, the people began to scatter in all directions. They formed different groups and nations, each with its own unique language. This event became known as the Tower of Babel.

Lesson: The story of the Tower of Babel reminds us of the importance of humility. The people in this story were so focused on their own glory and ambitions that they lost sight of God's plan for their lives. Their pride and disobedience led to confusion and division. We learn from this story the value of being humble, working together, and respecting one another's differences. It also teaches us the importance of seeking God's guidance in our lives and recognizing that our pride can lead us down the wrong path.

Abraham and Sarah

Genesis 12-21

A Journey of Faith

A long time ago, in a land called Ur, there lived a man named Abraham and his wife, Sarah. They were a kind and faithful couple, but there was one thing missing from their lives: they had no children.

One day, God spoke to Abraham and said, "I will make you the father of a great nation, and your descendants will be as numerous as the stars in the sky." Abraham was old, and Sarah was too, but they trusted God's promise.

Years passed, and they still had no children. Sarah thought she was too old to have a baby, so she told Abraham to have a child with her maidservant, Hagar. They had a son, Ishmael, but this wasn't God's plan.

God appeared to Abraham again and said, "No, Sarah will have a son, and you will name him Isaac." When Sarah heard this, she laughed because she couldn't believe it. But God's promise came true, and Sarah gave birth to Isaac.

Isaac grew up to be a joyful and blessed child. He brought much happiness to Abraham and Sarah in their old age. They learned that God keeps His promises, even when things seem impossible.

Lesson: The story of Abraham and Sarah teaches us about faith and trusting in God's promises. They waited patiently for God's plan to unfold, even when it seemed impossible. We learn that God's timing is perfect, and His promises always come true.

Joseph's Colorful Coat

Genesis 37-50

Dreams, Deceit, and God's Redemption

In the ancient land of Canaan, there lived a young man named Joseph, known for his special gift of dream interpretation. He was the beloved son of his father, Jacob, who showed his affection by gifting Joseph a magnificent, colorful coat. This coat became a symbol of his father's love and made his brothers exceedingly jealous.

The jealousy in Joseph's family reached a breaking point when his brothers decided to take a drastic step. They sold Joseph as a slave to traders bound for Egypt. It was a heart-wrenching separation, and Joseph found himself in a foreign land with no knowledge of his family's whereabouts.

In Egypt, Joseph's life took another painful turn. Falsely accused of a crime he did not commit, he was unjustly imprisoned. Despite his difficult circumstances, Joseph remained faithful to God and used his gift of dream interpretation to help fellow inmates.

Eventually, Joseph's ability to interpret dreams led him to an encounter with the Pharaoh of Egypt. The Pharaoh had a perplexing dream, and Joseph's interpretation not only foretold a future of seven years of plenty but also seven years of severe famine. Impressed by Joseph's wisdom, Pharaoh appointed him as a high-ranking official, responsible for storing food during the years of abundance. As the years of famine arrived, Joseph's own family, including his brothers, came to Egypt in search of food. Unrecognizable to them, Joseph revealed his identity and forgave them for their past wrongs. The family was joyously reunited, showing the remarkable power of forgiveness and reconciliation.

Lesson: Joseph's story beautifully illustrates the power of forgiveness, faithfulness, and how God can turn challenging circumstances into something good. Despite enduring hardship and betrayal, Joseph forgave his brothers and reunited with his family, exemplifying the profound impact of forgiveness and reconciliation in our lives.

Moses in the River

Exodus 1-14

God's Protective Hand

Long ago, in the land of Egypt, there lived a kind-hearted woman named Jochebed, who was from the tribe of Levi. Jochebed had a precious baby boy, whom she named Moses. Moses was born during a time when the Pharaoh of Egypt was worried about the growing number of Israelite people.

To protect her baby from harm, Jochebed made a special basket, waterproofed it, and gently placed Moses in it. With a heavy heart, she set the basket afloat in the river, trusting that God would watch over her son.

Miraculously, the basket floated safely along the river's current and eventually came to rest near the Pharaoh's palace. Pharaoh's daughter, who was bathing in the river, discovered the baby and felt compassion for him. She decided to adopt Moses as her own.

As Moses grew, he became a wise and strong young man. One day, he witnessed an Egyptian mistreating an Israelite, and he defended his fellow Israelite. Fearing for his life, Moses fled into the wilderness, where he encountered God at the burning bush. God called Moses to lead the Israelites out of Egypt.

With God's guidance, Moses returned to Egypt and, through many miracles, led the Israelites out of slavery. He parted the Red Sea, and God protected them on their journey through the desert.

Lesson: Moses' story teaches us about God's protective hand and how He can use ordinary people to do extraordinary things. It also reminds us of the importance of trust and faith, even in the face of difficult circumstances.

The Plagues of Egypt

Exodus 7-12

A Testament to God's Miraculous Might

In the ancient land of Egypt, a momentous battle of wills transpired. Moses, acting as the determined advocate for his people, the Israelites, stood before the imposing Pharaoh, beseeching the release of the Israelites from the chains of slavery. However, Pharaoh's heart remained as unyielding as the towering pyramids that graced his kingdom.

In response to Pharaoh's unwavering obstinacy, God, in His boundless power and infinite wisdom, initiated a series of extraordinary events known as the Ten Plagues. These were not merely punitive measures; they were awe-inspiring manifestations of divine authority, meticulously orchestrated to demonstrate God's supreme power and sway Pharaoh's implacable resolve.

These divine wonders included rivers turning to blood, the land being overrun by frogs, swarms of gnats or lice emerging from the dust, hordes of flies, a devastating disease striking the Egyptian livestock, the painful affliction of boils and sores, a catastrophic hailstorm, locust invasions consuming all remaining vegetation, an impenetrable darkness that shrouded Egypt, and, ultimately, the heart-wrenching loss of the firstborn in every Egyptian household.

These divine acts were not only demonstrations of God's supreme power but profound lessons as well. They embodied the unwavering commitment of the Almighty to shield and emancipate His chosen people from the oppressive yoke of slavery.

Lesson: The story of the Plagues of Egypt, with its awe-inspiring displays of God's miraculous signs, serves as a testament to His relentless determination to liberate His people. It underscores the significance of faith, obedience, and the ultimate fulfillment of God's divine plan, even in the face of seemingly insurmountable challenges.

Crossing the Red Sea

Genesis 14

Israel's Escape and the Power of God's Path

Following the ten devastating plagues, Pharaoh, the ruler of Egypt, finally relented, allowing the Israelites to depart. Their journey to freedom led them to the shores of the Red Sea, a seemingly insurmountable obstacle.

With uncertainty in their hearts, the Israelites faced a test of faith. In this moment of need, God revealed His plan. He instructed Moses to stretch out his hand, and a mighty wind began to blow. The waters of the Red Sea miraculously parted, unveiling a dry path in the midst of the sea.

In an act of faith and courage, the Israelites ventured onto the dry seabed, walking between towering walls of water. The pursuing Egyptian army, which had initially released them but then pursued, followed the Israelites into the sea.

However, God, in His divine justice, protected His chosen people. When the Israelites reached the far shore, the sea closed, submerging the Egyptian chariots and soldiers. It was a miraculous deliverance.

With hearts full of gratitude, the Israelites sang songs of praise, acknowledging God's unfailing guidance and protection. Their journey continued, fueled by the knowledge that God would lead them to the Promised Land.

Lesson: The story of Crossing the Red Sea teaches us the importance of trusting God's path, even when faced with daunting obstacles. With unwavering faith, God can make a way where it seems impossible.

The Battle of Jericho

Joshua 6

Marching, Trumpets, and God's Divine Victory

The Israelites, after forty years of wandering in the wilderness, stood at the threshold of the Promised Land. Their new leader, Joshua, faced an imposing challenge as they approached the city of Jericho. This ancient city was known for its formidable walls, which seemed utterly impervious to any human effort. But, as always, God had a divine plan.

God spoke to Joshua, instructing him on a strategy that defied conventional wisdom. The plan was as remarkable as it was unconventional. For six days, the Israelites were to march around the city, once a day, in complete silence. In the procession were seven priests, each carrying a trumpet made from a ram's horn. On the seventh day, they were to march around Jericho seven times, and when the priests blew their trumpets, the people were to shout with all their might.

With unwavering faith, Joshua conveyed God's instructions to the Israelites. They followed this divine plan, walking around the city as directed. On the seventh day, as the seven priests blew their trumpets and the people shouted, a profound miracle unfolded before their eyes. The mighty walls of Jericho, which had stood as a symbol of insurmountable strength, began to crumble and fall. The city's defenses were rendered powerless against the divine might of God.

The city was conquered, and the Israelites stood in awe of the incredible power of God's strategy. It was a powerful reminder that, in the face of challenges that seem insurmountable, trusting in God's guidance and wisdom can lead to triumphant outcomes.

Lesson: The story of Joshua and Jericho is a testament to the importance of trusting God's strategy, even when faced with the most formidable obstacles. It teaches us that with unwavering faith, we can overcome challenges that may appear invincible through human strength alone.

Ruth and Naomi

Book of Ruth

Loyalty and Love

In the land of Bethlehem, a woman named Naomi faced a series of tragedies. Famine forced her family to leave their homeland for the land of Moab. There, her husband and two sons passed away, leaving her alone with her daughters-in-law, Orpah and Ruth.

Naomi decided to return to Bethlehem, and she encouraged her daughters-in-law to stay in Moab and find new husbands. Orpah chose to stay, but Ruth's love and loyalty for Naomi were unwavering. She uttered these touching words: "Where you go, I will go, and where you stay, I will stay. Your people will be my people, and your God my God."

Ruth and Naomi arrived in Bethlehem, and Ruth's dedication and hard work in the fields caught the attention of a man named Boaz. He was a close relative of Naomi's and had the right to marry Ruth. Boaz and Ruth eventually married, and their union brought joy and prosperity to both Ruth and Naomi.

Through Ruth's loyalty and love, Naomi's life was transformed from one of despair to one filled with hope and happiness. Their story serves as a beautiful example of the power of love and faithfulness.

Lesson: The story of Ruth and Naomi teaches us about loyalty, love, and the transformative power of unwavering commitment to family. It shows how acts of love and devotion can bring about hope and blessings even in the most challenging circumstances.

The Call of Samuel

1 Samuel 3:1-21

Listening to God's Voice

In a time when the words of the Lord were rare, and visions were not widespread, there lived a young boy named Samuel. He served in the house of the Lord under the care of a priest named Eli.

Each night, as Samuel lay near the Ark of the Covenant in the sacred temple, he heard a voice calling his name, "Samuel." It was a gentle, yet persistent voice, one that seemed to come from the depths of his soul.

Thinking it was Eli, the old priest, Samuel rushed to him. "Eli, here I am. You called me," he said.

Eli, realizing something divine was unfolding, told Samuel, "I did not call you, my son. Go back and lie down."

This happened several times, with Samuel rushing to Eli each time he heard the voice. On the fourth occasion, Eli instructed Samuel, "Go, lie down, and if he calls you, you shall say, 'Speak, Lord, for your servant is listening.'"

Samuel followed Eli's advice, and when the voice called again, he answered, "Speak, Lord, for your servant is listening."

In that moment, the presence of the divine enveloped Samuel. The Lord spoke to him, revealing messages and prophecies of great importance. Samuel's heart and ears were open, and he listened attentively. His life was forever changed.

As the years passed, Samuel grew to be a great prophet, renowned for his ability to hear and faithfully deliver God's messages to the people of Israel. His story is a testament to the power of listening to God's voice.

Lesson: The story of Samuel teaches us to be attentive to God's voice and open our hearts to His divine guidance.

King Solomon

1 Kings 1:11

The Wise King

Solomon, the son of the esteemed King David, is celebrated for his exceptional wisdom—an extraordinary gift from God. His journey into the annals of history begins with a remarkable encounter with the divine.

In a dream, God appeared before Solomon, offering him an extraordinary proposition: "Ask for whatever you want, and I will give it to you." While many rulers might have sought riches, power, or a lengthy life, Solomon's response was marked by humility and a profound desire for wisdom. Yet, he didn't seek just any wisdom. He beseeched God for the wisdom to govern his people justly, to distinguish right from wrong, and to make decisions steeped in fairness, wisdom, and compassion.

God, gratified by Solomon's selfless request, not only bestowed upon him unparalleled wisdom but also graced him with immense wealth, honor, and prosperity that surpassed the riches of any king of his time. Solomon's wisdom was soon put to the test in a scenario that would exemplify his deep understanding of human nature and his commitment to justice.

Solomon's wisdom was famously tested when two women claimed the same baby. He suggested dividing the child, but the real mother selflessly gave up her claim to save the baby, revealing her true identity.

Lesson: The story of King Solomon imparts a profound lesson about the importance of seeking wisdom and making just choices. It underscores that genuine wisdom extends beyond knowledge and encompasses acts of love, compassion, and justice. Solomon's wisdom reminds us that, with divine guidance, we can make choices that lead to justice and prosperity for ourselves and our communities.

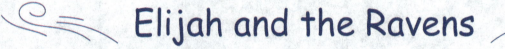

Elijah and the Ravens

1 Kings 17:2-6

God's provision

In a land plagued by drought, there lived a faithful man named Elijah. He was a prophet, chosen by God to deliver important messages to the people of Israel.

It was a time of great hardship in the land of Israel. The land was dry, and the people were hungry. There was a terrible drought, and the rivers and streams had run dry. The fields were brown, and there was little food to be found.

Elijah, too, felt the pangs of hunger. But he never lost his faith in God's love and care. He knew that God would provide for him, even in the toughest of times.
One day, as Elijah sat by a brook, he prayed to God for food. He asked God for help, and God listened. You see, God had a special plan to provide for Elijah during this time of drought.

As Elijah prayed, something incredible happened. Ravens, large black birds, began to appear in the sky. They circled above him, and to his amazement, they carried something in their beaks. It was food! These ravens, God's messengers, brought bread and meat to Elijah every morning and evening.
Elijah was astounded by God's provision. He drank from the brook and ate the food brought to him by the ravens. It was a miraculous act of love and care from God.

Days turned into weeks, and weeks into months, and still, the ravens came faithfully. Elijah never went hungry, and he knew that God was watching over him. Eventually, the brook dried up due to the prolonged drought, and God had another plan for Elijah. He sent Elijah to a kind widow in the town of Zarephath. There, God continued to work miracles through Elijah, showing His incredible love and provision.

Lesson: God's love and care for us can be seen in the most unexpected places and through the most unexpected messengers. Even in the toughest times, trust that He will provide for you, just as He did for Elijah.

Samson the Strong

Judges 13-16

Strength and Betrayal

In the land of ancient Israel, there lived a man named Samson, known for his extraordinary strength—a divine gift from God. Samson's incredible physical power was matched only by his ability to lead the Israelites against their enemies, the Philistines.

Samson's remarkable story began with a divine promise. Before his birth, an angel appeared to his mother, announcing that she would bear a son who would deliver the Israelites from the Philistine oppression. The condition of this divine blessing was that Samson would live as a Nazirite, a person consecrated to God from birth, and he must never cut his hair.

From his youth, Samson's strength was evident. He tore a lion apart with his bare hands and defeated a group of Philistine warriors. However, Samson's strength was rivaled by his weakness—his inability to resist the temptations of his heart.

Samson fell in love with Delilah, a Philistine woman. The Philistine rulers bribed her to discover the source of Samson's strength. Three times, Samson deceived Delilah by telling her false ways to subdue him. Yet, his heart and trust in her eventually led him to reveal the truth. As he slept with his head resting in Delilah's lap, she ordered a servant to shave his hair. Samson's strength was gone, and the Philistines captured him, gouging out his eyes.

In captivity, Samson's hair slowly grew back, and with it, his strength returned. During a great gathering of the Philistine rulers, he was brought to entertain them. With one last burst of strength, Samson pushed apart the pillars of the temple, causing it to collapse, killing both himself and his enemies.

Lesson: Samson's story serves as a powerful reminder of the importance of staying true to one's divine calling and resisting temptation. His strength and weakness highlight the consequences of straying from one's path, even with the most extraordinary gifts.

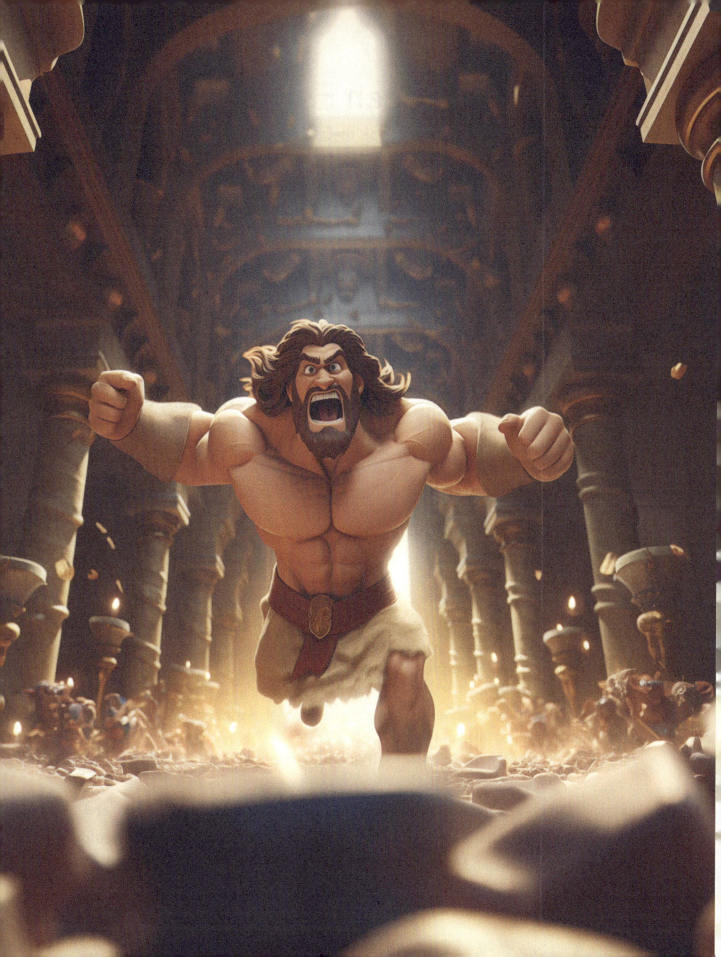

Queen Esther

Book of Esther

The Brave Queen

In the ancient kingdom of Persia, there lived a young Jewish woman named Esther. Her life was marked by courage and unwavering faith in God, and her story is a testament to how one person's bravery can change the course of history.

Esther was an orphan, raised by her cousin Mordecai. She lived in the capital city of Susa during the reign of King Xerxes. Despite her challenging circumstances, Esther was known for her beauty and grace.

The turning point in Esther's life came when King Xerxes sought a new queen, and Esther, by God's providence, was chosen. However, her heritage as a Jew was a closely guarded secret. Mordecai, who remained devoted to Esther, advised her to keep her identity hidden.

Soon, a crisis unfolded in the kingdom. A high-ranking official named Haman plotted to annihilate the Jewish people. Mordecai implored Esther to reveal her true identity to the king and seek his intervention. Esther, recognizing the grave danger her people faced, summoned her courage and arranged a banquet where she would make her appeal to the king.

At the crucial moment, Esther disclosed her heritage to the king and pleaded for her people's lives. The king, who held great affection for Esther, was moved to action. Haman's wicked plot was thwarted, and the Jewish people were spared.

Esther's faith in God and her bravery in the face of danger saved her people from destruction. Her story is celebrated during the Jewish festival of Purim, a time of rejoicing and remembering how faith and courage can lead to victory.

Lesson: Queen Esther's story teaches us the importance of courage and faith, even in the most challenging circumstances. It reminds us that we should stand up for what is right and just, even when it requires great bravery.

David and Goliath

1 Samuel 17

The Unlikely Hero

In the time of ancient Israel, a mighty giant named Goliath terrorized the land. He was a Philistine warrior, known for his immense size and strength, and he challenged the Israelites to a battle. The entire Israelite army trembled in fear, but a young shepherd named David stepped forward, armed with nothing but his faith and courage.

David was the youngest of his brothers and was often underestimated because of his youth. However, he possessed a deep faith in God and a profound understanding of the power of trust and bravery. When he heard Goliath's taunts and saw the fear in his people's eyes, he decided to face the giant.

Gathering only a sling and a few stones, David approached the battlefield, ready to confront the Philistine giant. His true strength lay not in physical might but in his unwavering faith. David knew that with God at his side, he could overcome the seemingly insurmountable challenge before him.

As the battle commenced, David stood his ground, loaded his sling, and with unwavering faith, he aimed and released a single stone. The stone found its mark, striking Goliath in the forehead. The mighty giant fell to the ground, defeated.

David's victory was not only a triumph of physical courage but also of deep faith. He trusted in God to guide his aim and protect him from the fearsome giant. His story has since become an enduring symbol of courage in the face of seemingly insurmountable odds.

Lesson: The story of David and Goliath teaches us that true courage and faith can overcome even the most daunting challenges. It reminds us that no obstacle is too great when we trust in a higher power and believe in ourselves.

Daniel's Daring Faith

Daniel 6

Daniel in the Lion's Den

In the great kingdom of Babylon, there lived a man named Daniel. He was known for his unwavering faith in God and his exceptional wisdom. Daniel's story is one of courage, faith, and trust in the face of adversity.

At the time, King Darius ruled over Babylon, and he recognized Daniel's wisdom and integrity. As a result, Daniel held a prominent position in the kingdom. This, however, aroused the jealousy of some of the king's officials, who plotted against Daniel.

They convinced King Darius to issue a decree that forbade anyone from praying to any god or human except the king for 30 days. Daniel, steadfast in his faith, continued to pray to God as he always had, defying the king's decree. When the conspirators caught him in the act, they reported his disobedience to the king.

Despite his admiration for Daniel, King Darius had no choice but to enforce his own decree, and he ordered Daniel to be thrown into a den of hungry lions. It seemed that Daniel's unwavering faith had led him to a perilous end.

That night, King Darius could not sleep, troubled by what had transpired. At the break of dawn, he rushed to the lion's den and called out to Daniel. To everyone's amazement, Daniel responded. He had been unharmed, as God had sent an angel to protect him from the lions.

Daniel's survival was a testament to his unyielding trust in God. The king recognized the greatness of the God whom Daniel served, and he decreed that all the people of his kingdom should revere the God of Daniel.

Lesson: The story of Daniel in the lion's den teaches us the importance of trusting in God, even in the face of adversity and danger. It reminds us that faith and unwavering trust can lead to miraculous outcomes, and that God's protection is a source of comfort and strength in challenging times.

Jonah and the Big Fish

Jonah 1-4

From Rebellion to Repentance

The story of Jonah is a tale of obedience, mercy, and the unrelenting love of God. Jonah was a prophet in ancient Israel, called by God to deliver a message to the people of Nineveh.

However, Jonah had other plans. He was hesitant to obey God's command and decided to flee in the opposite direction, boarding a ship headed for Tarshish. But God's plans are not so easily thwarted.

While at sea, a violent storm erupted, threatening the lives of everyone on board. Jonah, realizing that he was the cause of the tempest, told the crew to throw him overboard. Reluctantly, they did so, and Jonah was swallowed by a great fish, where he remained for three days and three nights.

Inside the belly of the fish, Jonah prayed to God for mercy. Recognizing his disobedience, he vowed to obey God's command and deliver the message to Nineveh. In response to his repentance, God ordered the fish to spew Jonah onto dry land.

Jonah, now willing to carry out God's mission, journeyed to Nineveh and delivered the message of repentance. To his surprise, the people of Nineveh, from the king to the commoners, heeded his words and turned from their wicked ways. God's mercy had prevailed, and He spared the city from destruction.

Lesson: Jonah's story teaches us about the importance of obedience to God's call and the boundless mercy and love of the Divine. It illustrates that no matter how far we may stray, God's compassion is always ready to welcome us back.

The Birth of Jesus

Matthew 2:1-12

The Savior's Arrival

More than two thousand years ago, in the tranquil town of Bethlehem, a momentous event unfolded. Mary and Joseph, a modest couple from Nazareth, journeyed to Bethlehem due to a decree from Caesar Augustus, who had called for a census across the vast Roman Empire.

Bethlehem presented an unexpected challenge; there were no rooms available in the inns. With no other option, they sought shelter in a humble stable. Here, amidst the simplicity of a stable, Mary gave birth to a baby boy, whom they named Jesus. Wrapped in swaddling clothes, He was nestled in a manger, a feeding trough meant for animals. It was in this unassuming setting that the Savior of the world made His entrance.

On that sacred night, a brilliant star illuminated the heavens, guiding shepherds and wise men to the miraculous birthplace. Shepherds, visited by a host of angels, became the first to witness the birth of the Savior and eagerly shared the extraordinary news.

The wise men, following the guiding star, embarked on a journey to Bethlehem, bearing gifts of gold, frankincense, and myrrh. These precious offerings symbolized their recognition of the divine and regal nature of the newborn child.

The birth of Jesus marked the fulfillment of ancient prophecies and the dawn of a new era. He came into the world to bring salvation, hope, and love to all of humanity, leaving an indelible mark on the course of history.

Lesson: The birth of Jesus encapsulates the essence of hope and love, revealing that even in the most unassuming of circumstances, a divine purpose can be fulfilled. It serves as a poignant reminder of the profound significance of faith, love, and the message of salvation that Jesus brought to the world.

Jesus and the Children

Matthew 19 & 21

Welcoming All

During His days of teaching and healing, a heartwarming story of Jesus and the children unfolded. Parents, with hope and joy, brought their little ones to Him, seeking His blessings and love. But as the children gathered around, the disciples, in their haste, tried to shoo them away, thinking they were a distraction.

Jesus, with a gentle and loving smile, saw what was happening. He turned to His disciples and said, "Let the little children come to me, and do not hinder them, for the kingdom of heaven belongs to such as these."

With those words, He opened His arms, inviting the children closer. Their innocent eyes sparkled with wonder as they approached Him, unaware of the vastness of His love. Jesus tenderly embraced each child, His hands resting on their heads as He offered His heartfelt blessings.

In a different moment, children in the temple began to sing songs of praise to Jesus, their voices filled with joy and adoration. However, this pure and beautiful display of devotion stirred some displeasure among the religious leaders. They questioned Jesus, asking if He heard what the children were saying.

With a compassionate tone, Jesus replied by quoting Scripture: "From the lips of children and infants, you, Lord, have called forth your praise."

The temple echoed with the sweet melodies of the children, and their voices became a living testament to the purity of their faith and their love for the Teacher.

Lesson: The stories of Jesus and the children remind us of the beauty of childlike faith, of hearts open to God's love, and of the importance of approaching God with simplicity and trust.

Feeding the Multitude

Matthew 14:13-21

A Miraculous Feast

Once upon a time, in a quiet place near the Sea of Galilee, a large crowd had gathered around Jesus. They had journeyed from near and far to hear His teachings and witness His miraculous healings. As the day wore on, their stomachs began to grumble, for they had been with Jesus for hours, and there was no food to be found.

Jesus, filled with compassion for the hungry multitude, turned to His disciples and said, "We must feed them." The disciples, perplexed by the vast number of people and the scarcity of food, wondered how they could accomplish this task.

Amidst the crowd, a young boy stepped forward. He had with him five small loaves of bread and two fish. It seemed like an insignificant offering in the face of such a great need, but the boy's willingness to share touched Jesus's heart.

Taking the loaves and fish, Jesus looked up to heaven and offered a prayer of blessing. Then, He broke the bread into pieces and divided the fish. The disciples began to distribute the miraculously multiplying food to the crowd.

As they went from person to person, the loaves and fish seemed never-ending. The multitude ate their fill, and there were even leftovers, filling twelve baskets. It was a wondrous and heartwarming moment, a feast provided by the hand of Jesus.

The people rejoiced not only for the satisfying meal but also for the incredible miracle they had witnessed. They realized that Jesus was not only a great teacher and healer but also a provider who could meet their deepest needs.

Lesson: The story of the feeding of the multitude reminds us that Jesus has the power to multiply blessings and provide for our needs, even when it seems impossible. Just as He fed the hungry crowd that day, He can fill our lives with abundance and compassion.

The Good Samaritan

Luke 10:30-37

A Lesson in Neighborly Love

Once upon a time, in the land of Israel, a traveler set out on a journey from Jerusalem to Jericho. As he made his way through the rocky and treacherous terrain, he fell victim to a group of robbers. They beat him, took his belongings, and left him wounded and helpless on the side of the road.

Soon, a priest passed by, heading down the same road. He saw the injured man but walked past on the other side, perhaps fearing ceremonial impurity or being too busy to offer help.

Then, a Levite, a religious figure, came upon the scene. Like the priest, he saw the wounded traveler but chose to continue his journey without extending a helping hand.

Hope seemed lost for the wounded man, lying in pain. But then, an unexpected Samaritan appeared. Samaritans and Jews had a history of conflict, but this compassionate Samaritan didn't let that stop him. He approached the injured man, bound his wounds, poured oil and wine on them, and placed him on his own animal. The Samaritan took the injured traveler to an inn and cared for him through the night.

The following day, the Samaritan gave money to the innkeeper, instructing him to look after the injured man and promising to return to pay any additional expenses.

The story of the Good Samaritan reminds us that compassion knows no boundaries. It teaches us that it's not just our friends and neighbors we should love and care for but also those in need, even if they seem different from us. Jesus told this story to illustrate the true meaning of loving one's neighbor.

Lesson: The Good Samaritan's story serves as a powerful lesson in compassion and loving our neighbors. It encourages us to help those in need, regardless of their background or circumstances.

The Prodigal Son

Luke 15:11-32

A Father's Unconditional Love

In a distant land, a wealthy man had two sons. The younger son, restless and eager to explore the world, approached his father and asked for his share of the inheritance. Though it was unusual to divide the inheritance while the father still lived, the father agreed, and the younger son set off for a distant country.

In that far-off land, the young man squandered his wealth in reckless living. Soon, a famine struck the land, and he found himself in dire need. He took a job feeding pigs but was so hungry that he longed to eat the pig's food.

In a moment of clarity, he realized his mistake and remembered the love of his father. He decided to return home, even if it meant becoming a servant in his father's house.

As he journeyed back, his father saw him from a distance and ran to embrace him, overwhelmed with joy at his return. The son confessed his mistakes and asked to be a servant. But his father would have none of it. He ordered a celebration, saying, "For this son of mine was dead and is alive again; he was lost and is found." The whole household rejoiced, and they prepared a great feast.

The elder son, who had remained loyal and responsible, was puzzled by the extravagant celebration. But his father explained, "We had to celebrate and be glad because this brother of yours was dead and is alive again; he was lost and is found."

This parable, known as the Prodigal Son, illustrates the boundless love and forgiveness of God. It reminds us that, no matter our past mistakes, when we turn to God with a repentant heart, He welcomes us with open arms.

Lesson: The Prodigal Son story teaches us about the depth of God's love and forgiveness. It encourages us to seek reconciliation and return to Him, no matter how far we may have strayed.

Jesus Walks on Water

Matthew 14:22-33

Stormy Seas & Fearless Faith

One evening, after a day of teaching and performing miracles, Jesus sent His disciples ahead in a boat to cross the Sea of Galilee. As night fell, the disciples found themselves battling strong winds and waves.

In the midst of the storm, they saw Jesus walking on the water. Fearful, they thought it was a ghost. But Jesus reassured them, saying, "Take courage! It is I. Don't be afraid."

Peter, filled with faith, asked to walk on water too. Jesus agreed, and Peter stepped out of the boat. At first, he walked on water, defying nature. The thrill of this miraculous moment filled his heart with wonder.

However, as Peter looked around and saw the howling wind and towering waves, fear overcame him. Doubt crept in, and he began to sink beneath the churning sea. Desperation in his voice, he cried, "Lord, save me!"

Without hesitation, Jesus reached out His hand and caught Peter. Their eyes locked, and the Savior's grip was firm. Together, they walked back to the boat, step by step. The moment they stepped into the boat, the storm ceased, and the sea became calm.

The disciples, with awe and gratitude in their hearts, worshiped Jesus, saying, "Truly you are the Son of God."

This story of Jesus walking on water and Peter's attempt to do the same is a testament to the power of faith and the significance of keeping our focus on Christ, even in life's most tempestuous moments.

Lesson: The story of Jesus walking on water teaches us the importance of unwavering faith in the midst of life's challenges. It reminds us that when we keep our eyes on Christ, we can overcome seemingly insurmountable obstacles.

The Good Shepherd

John 10:1-18

Lost & Found

In the heart of the Holy Land, where rolling hills and lush pastures stretched as far as the eye could see, a shepherd tended to his flock of sheep. Among these sheep was a special bond, a connection between the shepherd and his charges that ran deep.

This shepherd was no ordinary one; he was a reflection of the divine love and care of our Lord. Each day, he led his sheep to fresh pastures, ensuring they had plenty to eat and drink. He watched over them, protecting them from danger, whether it was a lurking wolf or a treacherous terrain.

And when one of his sheep went astray, the Good Shepherd would leave the ninety-nine in the safety of the fold and search tirelessly for the one that had wandered off. When he found the lost sheep, he would joyfully carry it back to the flock, rejoicing in the reunion.

This shepherd's love for his sheep was a glimpse into the love God has for His people. In the Bible, Jesus identified Himself as the Good Shepherd, who knows His sheep by name, lays down His life for them, and leads them to eternal life.

The story of the Good Shepherd reminds us of the loving and caring nature of our Savior. It teaches us that we are His cherished flock, and He will always seek out the lost and guide us to the safety of His love.

Lesson: The story of the Good Shepherd teaches us about the boundless love and care of Jesus for His people. It illustrates that we are cherished by Him, and He will seek out and save those who are lost.

The Baptism of Jesus

Matthew 3:13-17

Sinless Savior

In the ancient land of Judea, near the banks of the Jordan River, a significant event took place that marked the beginning of Jesus's earthly ministry. It was a moment of profound importance and symbolism—the baptism of Jesus by John the Baptist.

John, a humble and devoted preacher, had been calling people to repentance and baptizing them in the river as a sign of their cleansing from sin. Crowds flocked to him, seeking spiritual renewal. Among those who came to John was Jesus, the Son of God, sinless and blameless.

John was initially hesitant, feeling unworthy to baptize Jesus. He recognized the divine nature of the One who stood before him. But Jesus insisted, saying, "Let it be so now; it is proper for us to do this to fulfill all righteousness."

As Jesus entered the waters of the Jordan, John immersed Him, and as He emerged, a profound event occurred. The heavens opened, and the Holy Spirit descended in the form of a dove, alighting upon Jesus. A voice from heaven declared, "This is my Son, whom I love; with him, I am well pleased."

The baptism of Jesus signified the beginning of His public ministry, marked by His obedience to God's plan for the salvation of humanity. It was a moment of affirmation, as God the Father confirmed Jesus as His beloved Son and the embodiment of His divine purpose.

This event carries a profound lesson for us. It shows the significance of obedience to God's will, the sanctifying power of baptism, and the divine affirmation of God's love for His children.

Lesson: The baptism of Jesus highlights the importance of obedience, the transformative power of baptism, and the assurance of God's love for those who follow His path.

Zacchaeus

Luke 19:1-10

A Story of Change

In bustling Jericho, a tax collector named Zacchaeus was both wealthy and despised. Being of short stature, he climbed a tree to catch a glimpse of Jesus, who was passing through the city. To everyone's astonishment, Jesus called him by name and requested to stay at his home.

Zacchaeus, deeply moved by this encounter, joyfully welcomed Jesus into his home. This act of hospitality and humility demonstrated a profound change within Zacchaeus's heart. The people, however, grumbled, saying, "He has gone to be the guest of a sinner."

Yet, in the presence of Jesus, something extraordinary happened. Zacchaeus made a life-altering declaration, saying, "Look, Lord! Here and now I give half of my possessions to the poor, and if I have cheated anybody out of anything, I will pay back four times the amount."

This moment of genuine repentance and the commitment to make amends for his wrongdoings resonated deeply with Jesus. He declared, "Today, salvation has come to this house because this man, too, is a son of Abraham."

Zacchaeus's story is a vivid illustration of the transformative power of encountering Jesus. In the midst of societal scorn and personal wealth, the presence of the Lord changed not only his actions but the very core of his being. His life became a testament to the grace and forgiveness offered by Jesus, and it serves as a powerful reminder that no one is beyond redemption.

Lesson: The story of Zacchaeus teaches us about the transformative power of encountering Jesus, the significance of genuine repentance, and the desire to make amends for past wrongdoings. It underscores the universal truth that no one is beyond the reach of God's grace.

The Miracle of Lazarus

John 11

Lazarus Lives Again

In the small village of Bethany, a family dear to Jesus lived: Lazarus, Martha, and Mary. They were not only His friends but also His devoted followers.

One day, Lazarus fell seriously ill, and his sisters sent a message to Jesus, saying, "Lord, the one you love is sick." However, Jesus did not immediately go to them. Instead, He stayed where He was for two more days. By the time He arrived in Bethany, Lazarus had been in the tomb for four days.

Martha, filled with sorrow, met Jesus and expressed her faith, saying, "Lord, if you had been here, my brother would not have died."

Jesus, deeply moved by the grief of those around Him, went to the tomb. He commanded that the stone be rolled away. Martha was concerned, as Lazarus had been dead for four days, and the stench of death would be overpowering.

But Jesus reminded her, "Did I not tell you that if you believe, you will see the glory of God?" As the stone was removed, Jesus prayed to the Father. Then, with a loud voice, He called, "Lazarus, come out!"

To the amazement of everyone present, Lazarus, still wrapped in burial cloths, emerged from the tomb. Jesus had performed a miracle—a resurrection from the dead.

The story of Lazarus's miraculous return to life teaches us about the power of Jesus over death. It reminds us that in our darkest moments, when hope seems lost, Jesus can bring life, hope, and transformation.

Lesson: The Miracle of Lazarus underscores the incredible power of Jesus over death and the importance of unwavering faith, even in the face of seemingly insurmountable circumstances.

The Golden Rule

Matthew 7:12

Treat Others as You Want to Be Treated

In the heart of Jesus's teachings lies a profound principle known as the Golden Rule. This rule is a simple yet powerful guide to how we should treat others.

Jesus said, "So in everything, do to others what you would have them do to you, for this sums up the Law and the Prophets."

The Golden Rule is a call to empathy and kindness. It encourages us to place ourselves in the shoes of others and consider how our actions might affect them. It is a universal principle that transcends cultural and religious boundaries, emphasizing the importance of love, compassion, and understanding.

By living according to the Golden Rule, we create a better world where kindness and love are the foundation of our interactions with others. It teaches us to treat everyone with respect and compassion, for we, too, desire the same treatment.

Lesson: The Golden Rule, as taught by Jesus, reminds us of the importance of treating others with the same love, kindness, and respect that we desire for ourselves. It is a timeless and universal principle that can guide us in our relationships and interactions with others.

Jesus Calms the Storm

Matthew 8:23-27

Trusting in Jesus

One day, as Jesus and His disciples embarked on a boat to cross the Sea of Galilee, an unexpected tempest descended upon them. The sky darkened, and the wind howled with fury. Towering waves crashed against the boat, threatening to swallow it whole. Panic gripped the disciples as water filled their vessel.

Amidst the chaos, Jesus remained seemingly undisturbed, peacefully asleep in the stern of the boat. His disciples, shaken to their core, woke Him in a state of desperation, crying out, "Master, save us! We're going to drown!"

With a calm and unwavering demeanor, Jesus arose and rebuked the fierce winds and the raging sea. Immediately, a profound transformation occurred—the storm ceased, and the once-turbulent sea transformed into a calm one. A profound peace enveloped them.

Turning to His disciples, Jesus posed a question that echoed through the ages, "Why are you so afraid? Do you still have no faith?"

The disciples, in awe of the power they had witnessed, began to understand that Jesus was not only their Teacher but also the Lord of creation itself. Even the wind and the waves obeyed His command.

Lesson: The account of Jesus calming the storm serves as a powerful illustration of the significance of having faith in Jesus. It teaches us that in the most turbulent moments of life, trusting in Him can bring a profound sense of peace and tranquility.

The Last Supper

Matthew 26:17-30

Sharing Bread and Wine

In the final days leading up to His crucifixion, Jesus shared a poignant and symbolic meal with His disciples, an event that has come to be known as the Last Supper. This meal was celebrated during the Passover festival, a significant Jewish holiday.

As Jesus and His disciples gathered in an upper room, He took bread and blessed it, then broke it and gave it to them, saying, "Take, eat; this is my body." He also took a cup, offered thanks, and gave it to them, saying, "Drink from it, all of you. This is my blood of the covenant, which is poured out for many for the forgiveness of sins."

This simple yet profound act of sharing bread and wine took on deep meaning. Jesus was using these elements to symbolize His impending sacrifice on the cross, where His body would be broken, and His blood shed for the forgiveness of sins. He was establishing a new covenant between God and humanity through His own sacrifice.

During the Last Supper, Jesus also revealed that one of His disciples would betray Him, and another would deny Him. This somber moment highlighted the human frailty and imperfection that Jesus had come to redeem through His sacrifice.

The Last Supper remains a central part of Christian tradition, commemorated as the Eucharist or Holy Communion. It serves as a reminder of the sacrifice Jesus made for the salvation of humanity and the new covenant He established.

Lesson: The Last Supper is a poignant reminder of Jesus's sacrificial love and the new covenant of forgiveness and grace He established. It also underscores the importance of humility and self-examination in our walk with God.

The Redemption

Matthew 27:32-66

The Crucifixion and Resurrection

The culmination of Jesus's earthly ministry was marked by the events of His crucifixion and resurrection, which form the heart of the Christian faith.

Betrayed by one of His own disciples, Jesus was arrested and subjected to a series of trials. He was ultimately sentenced to be crucified—a torturous and humiliating form of execution. He carried His own cross to Golgotha, the Place of the Skull, where He was nailed to the cross alongside two criminals.

During His crucifixion, darkness covered the land, and Jesus cried out, "My God, my God, why have you forsaken me?" After hours of agony, He yielded His spirit and died.

His body was taken down from the cross and placed in a tomb, sealed with a large stone. Guards were placed outside to prevent anyone from tampering with the tomb. It seemed that hope was lost, and Jesus's followers were left in grief.

However, on the third day, something extraordinary occurred. The tomb was found empty, and angels declared, "He is not here; he has risen, just as he said!" Jesus had triumphed over death, and His resurrection was a powerful testament to His divinity and the victory over sin and death.

The crucifixion and resurrection of Jesus are the cornerstones of the Christian faith. They symbolize His sacrificial love and the hope of eternal life for all who believe in Him.

Lesson: The crucifixion and resurrection of Jesus remind us of the depth of His love and the promise of salvation. It is a story of hope, redemption, and the triumph of life over death.

Prayers

Prayer is a powerful way to connect with God, to express gratitude for the blessings in our lives, and to seek strength and guidance in times of need. You don't need to use fancy words; simply speak from your heart. You can pray for your family, your friends, and for the strength to face challenges with the same courage and faith as the heroes in the Bible stories.

Here are a few prayers to get you started:

Thank You Prayer:
Thank you, God, for this brand new day, For guiding me along the way. Bless my family, bless my friends and keep me safe until the day ends.
Amen.

Mealtime Prayer:
God, thank you for this food we share, Keep us healthy and strong. Bless the hands that prepared this meal.
Amen.

Bedtime Prayer:
As I lay down to sleep, please watch over me and my loved ones. Bless us with sweet dreams and a fresh start in the morning.
Amen.

CLOSING THOUGHTS

As we conclude our journey through "Bible Stories For Kids: Timeless Tales of Faith and Courage," we want to leave you, our young readers, with the enduring lessons and inspiration these stories provide.

In the pages of this book, you've encountered remarkable accounts of courage, unwavering faith, and profound acts of love. The Bible is a treasury of timeless wisdom and guidance, and these stories exemplify the extraordinary ways in which God's hand shapes the lives of His people.

The tales you've explored are not confined to the past; they are meant to illuminate your present and guide your future. When you face challenges, remember the resilience of Noah, the trust of Abraham and Sarah, and the determination of David. In moments of uncertainty, reflect on Samuel's willingness to listen for God's voice.

The love, wisdom, and strength portrayed in these stories are always with you, just as they were with the heroes of these timeless tales. As you close this book, know that you are never alone; God's love surrounds you.

We hope these stories have filled you with inspiration, deepened your faith, and provided valuable guidance. Our wish is that the lessons you've learned will continue to light your path, bringing you closer to God's enduring wisdom and grace.

With this, we bid you good day, young reader, and may your days ahead be filled with the enduring lessons of faith and courage found in the pages of this book.

Made in the USA
Coppell, TX
22 November 2023

24580825R00044